GIRL WAKE UP

Bernadette Bolden

Fulton Books, Inc.
Meadville, PA

Published by Fulton Books 2020

ISBN 978-1-64654-141-6 (paperback)
ISBN 978-1-64654-142-3 (digital)

Printed in the United States of America

I would like to dedicate this book to my father, Wheeler Bolden Jr, who showed and taught me what a real man is.

Here are three things I want you to do while reading this book:

1. When you see the words *grown boy* in this book, please remember this—a grown boy is not a man. He may look like a grown man, but he is not.

   A grown boy will ask a woman for money, and he has no shame in doing this.

   A grown boy does not want to work, nor will he look for or go to work.

   A grown boy wants to come live with you rent-free while eating all your groceries, increasing your utility bills, and drive your car as if it were his.

   A grown boy will lie in your bed while you get up and go to work.

   A grown boy will leave you with a baby to take care of on your own.

   A grown boy will not admit to nor will he accept his responsibilities.

A grown boy will walk away when he gets ready, leaving you to pick up the broken pieces of your life alone and on your own.

This is my definition of a grown boy who thinks he is a man. Do not allow this grown boy to fool you. I am sure we all know at least one grown boy posing, pretending, and claiming to be a man.

2. When you see the word *man* in this book, remember, a man is self-sufficient.

A man will not ask a woman for money or hint around that he wants money from her.

A man will not ask a woman for anything because he takes care of himself.

A man will offer to help you and will help you but is not obligated to do so.

A man will not complicate your life by bringing you his drama or leave you with another mouth to feed alone.

A man will accept his responsibilities, and he will put your needs before his own.

A man will work as many jobs as necessary to be self-reliant.

A man will take care of a need when he sees one has risen in your life.

A man will not play with your heart or your emotions.

A man will be truthful to you even if the truth hurts you.

A man will keep his word to you, for he knows what it means to be a man of integrity.

3. Please read this book slowly and repeatedly until what you have read sinks in and is learned.

Read the difference between a grown boy and a man as many times as you need to until it sinks in deep so that when a male approaches you, you will know without a doubt if you are talking to a grown boy or a man.

THE SCREAM

*U**ggghhh.* Ladies, we all understand and are very familiar with this scream. No, I am not talking about the scream when you think that you have found your Prince Charming.

I am talking about when you meet someone, and he is very attractive; he has a job and says all the right things. He makes you believe he can reach the sun, moon, and stars and give them to you.

Then he opens his mouth after about fifteen or more of those late-night conversations. You know what conversations—the ones that make you feel like a teenager in love for the first time, the ones that make you want to shout to the world, "I found him, I finally found him," and you are so giddy and happy.

Then he goes and says some stupid things that make you want to scream and pull out your hair.

I know you were thinking about the scream of "I have finally found him," and I was not talking about that scream. Sorry, I got your hopes up and got you going, but I am talking about the scream of "Not again, another loser, and now I have to start all over again."

Yes, I am talking about this scream. The scream of frustration—now does this scream sound familiar? Now you are thinking, *Something is not right.* You most certainly are right; something smells very bad here.

Now your mind is racing, and you are thinking back to your first conversation with him, and you are saying to yourself, "I thought he said he had a job. Did he not tell me he had a job? Did he lie to me?"

Now the one eyebrow goes up, and you say, "Here we go again." You should have been paying attention to him instead of his good looks, and all those late-night conversations distracted you.

You should have also been paying very close attention to his financial and living situation, but you were busy floating on a cloud, and he brought you down to earth when he asked you for money. Now you are paying attention.

Ladies, some of you are a member like me. I am in the Sisterhood of Boy, Please, and the rest of you need to think about joining. There is no age limit; all you have to do is be born female. You are 100-percent guaranteed acceptance with no cost to you.

What is the Sisterhood of Boy, Please, you just asked? Let us venture into chapter two to find out.

THE SISTERHOOD
OF BOY, PLEASE

Here is my definition of the Sisterhood of Boy, Please. A grown boy pretends to be a man, who does not or will not work but has no problem asking you for money or if he can come live with you, and you have only known him for two days or one week.

He cannot contribute to your household and has no intentions on doing so. He will make your bills bigger and your refrigerator lighter by eating your groceries. This is when you say to him, "Boy, Please."

Now if you find yourself saying, "Boy, Please," a lot to a grown boy, it is time to kick that butt out of your life. Notice I did not say kick him out of your house. I said kick him out of your life. I said life because sometimes women, when you kick a grown boy out of your house, you might fall weak and let him back in the house.

As we all know, when you are sick and tired of being sick and tired and you kick a grown boy out of your life, he is out forever.

Ladies, listen for a moment. Most of you have fallen, and if you have not fallen, you will fall for that man who you thought was the one, only to find out not only was he not the one, but he could never be the one in a million, billion, or gazillion years.

If you are reading this book before you start to date, then you are very smart to do so. You will save yourself a lot of heartaches and headaches. You are very fortunate. Some of us had to go through it to learn what you are getting firsthand and free of emotional pain and damage.

I pray you really take heed to what you are reading and learning. Ladies, there are some early warning signs of this grown boy, and I will teach you these signs so you will be aware of him and will know to run from him, and run fast when he approaches you.

EARLY WARNING SIGN (ONE)

The Target

The definition of the word *target* is a person, object, or place selected as the aim of an attack. Remember this meaning of the word *target* as you read this chapter.

Read it again, write it down, or do whatever you have to do so long as you remember the definition of the word *target*. Now, here we go. Read on.

He sees you and you make eye contact, and you made the mistake of smiling at him, and he says under his breath or in his mind, "She is the one. Yes, she will do."

You think you have just made a connection, but what you have actually done was make one of the biggest mistakes in your life. Who are you to him? In his eyes, you are his next target.

You see, this grown boy targeted you because of something you have either said or done. Let me explain what I am saying. When this grown boy is holding a conversation with you, he is looking for certain words and body language.

If you are speaking in a not-so-assured voice, you are a target. If you put out vibes of being lonely, you are a target. If you let him know you are on the upward ladder, you are a big target.

If you display the need or desire to be married at the beginning of your conversation with him, you are a target. If you tell him of a windfall you just received or will be receiving (this includes your income tax check), you are a target.

Why did I say something about the income tax check? Because there is something out there known as income tax check pimping. This means your ex or a new grown boy in your life may have targeted you because he knows it is income tax season, and he knows you will have some money.

Therefore, he comes around, is nice, and acts like the best thing to you since sliced bread. Nevertheless, when your money is gone, he is gone.

Wake up, ladies. These men are out here, and their job is to find a target and hold on to it as long as they can and ride that wave all the way out.

Now, if you are a target or you just found out by reading this chapter that you are a target or if you think you are a target, read this chapter again and you will know and receive your answer.If your answer is yes and you just found out that you are a target, run and run fast from this person.

He never had your best interest in mind; he has always been and will always be about himself. Now consider yourself warned and educated, and for goodness' sake, girl, wake up.

EARLY WARNING SIGN (TWO)

The Beggar

Ladies, let me tell you something. There are grown boys out here (ooooow, child) that are professional beggars, and I do not mean for money or sex.

I mean, this grown boy knows he has acquired a great target (meaning you), and he knows he has not landed you yet, but he has to make sure he gets you before some other grown boy does. Now, if he has you, he must make sure that he keeps you.

Ladies, I tell you the absolute truth: you have not seen a grown boy beg like this one beg because he is sooooo good at it. Let me tell you why he is sooooo good at it.

It is because he realizes that if he does not acquire this target (meaning you), he will have to find a job and go to work. If he has spent some time trying to acquire you and he still has not, he will keep trying until he gets you.

You see, his objective is to not have to find a job or go to work. He just wants to sleep in your bed all day, sit on your furniture, play Xbox or PlayStation all day, eat your food, drive your car—let us not forget—talk on your phone or get on chat lines, and talk to other women while you go out the door to work.

Yes, I said get on chat lines and talk to other women. No, I have not had this happen to me, but I have met men off the chat line that were married or lived with a woman.

You see, you are working hard to make a living for yourself, and this grown boy, well, he is playing games and using you. I met a man off a chat line one day, and I realized that he only called me during the daytime hours, and I could never reach him at night.

If this sounds familiar to any of you, keep reading. I knew he had to be married or he lived with a woman. Either way, I do not play those kinds of games. I do believe in what goes around comes around.

When I get married, I do not want some woman playing with my husband, so I do not play around with anyone else's husband. If you are in a relationship with a married man, let me be the second person to tell you to stop because nothing good is going to come from that.

I said let me be the second person because I am sure someone else has told you that what you are doing is wrong, and it will only come back to hurt you later. It is time to stop believing his lies and move on with your life. Besides, have you not heard the saying, "A man that will cheat on his wife will cheat on you?" Believe me; it is true.

Now back to the grown boy, I was pissed that he lied to me, so I decided I would burst his bubble. "How did I burst his bubble?" you ask. I told his wife. "How did I let her know what he was doing?" you ask.

I called her housephone in the early morning hours. This guaranteed that she would answer the phone. (Ladies, we make sure we answer a phone ringing in our house after midnight.) I asked for him, and when she said, "Who is this?" I spilled the beans.

You see, this grown boy was so stupid; he called me one day from the housephone where she pays the bills, and I saved the number. Therefore, I knew it was my duty to make her aware, sound the alarm, and let this woman know what this grown boy was doing.

So often, we get mad at the other woman, but I was the other woman, and I did not know he was married, but

I had a feeling because of the hours I talked to him and could not reach him.

Therefore, I went to work questioning him and doing some investigating on my own. You see, this grown boy had some lies for me and will have some for you too, but when I found out, I dropped him as if he was a red-hot poker.

Now back to the beggar. This beggar has a plan, and he has been working on that thing all his life, and this is why he is such a professional beggar, honey. You thought it was because he was just so sincere. Ha! No, honey. Check his hands. See if they are soft as yours.

If so, he has not done a hard day's work in his life, other than chasing down targets. If by reading this chapter, you realized that you have a beggar in your home or are in a relationship with one, run and run fast from this grown boy.

In other words, get his butt far away from you as possible, and please do not keep falling for the lies. Girl, wake up.

EARLY WARNING
SIGN (THREE)

The Housekeeper and Cook

Now this grown boy has somehow entered your home by way of targeting you, or you just simply let him in. It does not matter how he got in. He is in, and like a pig in slop, he loves it. Allow me to enlighten you on how he got in and who he is.

One day you met a grown boy. You may have just simply been holding what you thought was a great conversation with this grown boy and said something like, "It would be nice to have a home-cooked meal and a clean house when I get home from work because I am so tired most of the time, and I cannot do it all." Then he heard the bell. *Ding-dong*, and it was not Avon calling.

That was your target bell he heard in his head go off, and poor, innocent you not knowing what you just said, you have been targeted. You had no idea who you just let in your home.

Giiiiiirl, now he is cooking as if he is Rachael Ray and cleaning your house as if he is Martha Stewart all the while thinking, *I am in, I made it inside*, and you had better believe he is telling his homeboys that.

You see, women, that was his goal—to get in your home, and in his mind, he is set for life or until you wake up. This is what I am praying and hoping this book do for you—wake you up and set you free.

He has no intentions on ever working or leaving your home. Why should he? He is perfectly content on being a grown boy, and if you do not make him step up and become a man, why should he? In his mind, he has the perfect setup for life.

Please be on the lookout also because if he has no job or means to support himself and you do, this grown boy may ask you to marry him, sealing and securing his position for life. Now if you realize you have a housekeeper and a cook in your home, run and run fast from this grown boy.

EARLY WARNING SIGN (FOUR)

The Winter Man (Grown Boy)

During the spring and summer months, the sun is shining, it is warm outside, and all is well in the eyes of the hunting grown boy. Wait. Winter is approaching, and so is he. "Who is he?" you ask. He is the winter man (grown boy).

He is the grown boy who approaches at the middle or near the end of summer. You see, he has to have a roof over his head and food in his belly for free during the winter months. Just like the bear, he only wants to sleep and eat at no cost to himself.

Therefore, he looks for women who say something like this: "I sure do not want to be alone another winter" or

"It would be nice to have someone to cuddle up with this winter." The winter man (grown boy) prefers women with children because he knows she will keep a roof over her children's head and food in their bellies, and she will do the same for him.

Now you do not have to have children. He just prefers them because it is like a million-dollar insurance policy for him. Ladies, if I teach you nothing else, I want to teach you the power of your words.

They will bring good or bad, positive or negative effects into your life. So watch out for the seasonal changes and this grown boy. If he approaches you and you do not see a car, honey, it is the bus.

Now there is nothing wrong with the bus if he actually uses it to get to work. Make sure to watch out for the grown boy who changes lines in the grocery store because he sees all the groceries you are buying, and he is only buying a package of doughnuts with change.

He may also try to be witty and say something like "What time is dinner?" Tell him it will be ready the day after never and ready when he pays for the groceries. If he pays for the groceries, well, you are on your own with that one. LOL. Be careful, women, what you say and to whom you say it because you may become a target for the winter man (grown boy).

Make no mistake about it; he is on the hunt, and if you are not careful, you will find yourself a target or, worse yet, involved with this grown boy because you did not want to be alone this winter. If you think you are talking to the winter man, run and run fast from this grown boy.

EARLY WARNING
SIGN (FIVE)

The Lover

Watch out because this grown boy is smooooooooooooth like a hot knife running through butter. He is a slow talker and a great listener as well as understanding, and he is the most dangerous one of them all.

Therefore, I will take my time on this chapter because I have had the experience of having one of these grown boys, playing his game, and shutting him down, and it was the most fun I have had in my life. This is where the phrase "Do not hate the player, hate the game" comes in, and he was the player and he was played.

When I first met him, he was romantic and a great listener. He worked forty hours a week, had a car, and came over whenever we wanted to spend time with each other. He was educated to a point, but I was still smarter than he was. Women are smarter than men are, but there are some intelligent men in this world, and I truly can appreciate them.

I thought everything was great, but something in my gut just would not let me go all in. (You understand when your gut feeling says, "Do not do that" or "You had better wait," you choose to listen or ignore it.) Well, I listened and waited. Meanwhile, we continued to spend time together and enjoy each other's company, and he wanted to start doing that r word—you know that *relationship* word—and so we did.

All the while, I was still on guard because something was just not right. Then that moment came—the moment when you look each other in the eyes—and we both decided as the song says ("seem like you ready to go all the way"), and we did. OMG, this grown boy was the best lover in the world as far as I was concerned, but do not get it twisted.

He was on cloud twenty, and I was on cloud fifteen. I am no joke in the bedroom. Come on, women. Some of us can toot our horns about the bedroom just like men toot their horns, but this is not about me.

Now, he has mentioned the m word—no, not the *marriage* word but *move*. He now wants us to move in together.

(Errr…) This is where I put on the breaks. I know some of you just said, "What is wrong with that? If you love each other and want to be together, what is wrong with moving in together?" Here is why.

1. God said it is wrong to do so, just as it was wrong for me to sleep with this man and we were not married yet.

2. We had not been dating long enough for us to decide that "now I want to be under the same roof with you 24/7." Besides, people can pretend for about six months. After that, the real them begins to come out.

3. He began to do some strange things. I am a very observant person, and I remember everything someone tells me.

I began to notice things like him calling me two to four times in the middle of the day when at first you were too busy to do that. All of a sudden, we could now do lunch dates when at first we could not.

Then he started asking for twenty dollars here and there until payday, which never came. So I said (and anyone that knows me know I do not beat around the bush), "You have been asking me for a lot of money lately. Have you lost your job?" This is what he said. Wait for it. Wait for it. Go.

He said, "No, I quit." I said, "You did what!" (Add that high tone in the voice. You know it was there.) He said, "I quit," as if that was okay to do in this economy.

I said, "I hope you are looking for another job." He said, "That is why I thought we could move in together because you are working and can support the both of us, and I can continue giving you this dick anytime you want it." LOL, yes, this clown said *dick*. OMG, I laughed so hard at him when he said that.

He did not see the humor in what he just said to me, so I had to point it out to him. I said, "You must be out your rabbit and (but I used the other word that starts with a and ends in ss) mind to think that I would ever support any man.

You must be out your rabbit a———— mind to think that you put it on me that good that I would allow you to come in my home unemployed." He had no chance employed getting in my home unless we were married, but unemployed, yeah right.

I also said to him, "I could go and buy a device—bigger, longer, thicker, and wider than you, that will perform better than you, perform and stop when I cut it off, without me having to feed it or have it lay in my bed watching my TV while I go to work."

Here is when you say no, not "Boy, please." You say *hell to* the *no*. Ladies, if this grown boy has entered your home by this measure, honey, do yourself a favor and get rid of that extra stomach you have to fill, and watch your grocery bill go down.

It is time that we as women start listening to our gut feelings and adhere to what it is telling us. No man should be in your life by this means because it is only a temporary fix.

One day you will wake up and realize all he is contributing to your household is sex, and then you will be like "Did I really settle for this? Did I really do this to myself?" Yes, you did. Listen to me when I say this: no one's sex is that good that you should allow a grown boy to lay up on you while you take care of him.

Please go back and read the difference between a man and a grown boy again. You can do bad or better by yourself. By the way, I do not own one of those devices, and neither should you. Keep yourself pure as Jesus would want you to for your husband, and He will send you your husband that He has chosen for you. You must wait on Jesus and not choose for yourself.

YOU MAY HAVE ONE

Ladies, I am going to tell you something later on in this chapter, but first, I am going to talk to you for a moment as real as I can because I love you. From one woman to another woman who loves herself too much to allow this to continue to happen to herself, I must tell you the truth in hopes that you will start loving yourself more as well.

You may be a woman who has, had, or still have one of these grown boys with multiple qualities as mentioned in the preceding chapters in your home. If so, please do not feel bad. Just be glad that you have been enlightened or, as I like to say, you just woke up.

Now I would suggest to you what to do next. Nevertheless, truly it is your choice; this is why I said I would suggest to you what to do next. You must get this grown boy out of your house if you are not married to him, and if you are, I will discuss what to do if you are married to one in the next chapter.

How can he ever call himself a man if you are hindering his growth by not allowing Jesus to grow him up as a man? He must leave your home. He is blocking many of your blessings from God just by being in your home.

If you do not believe me, put him out and see if you and your entire household do not come up in blessings. The reason I said household is because there are women out there with children who has this grown boy in their home.

In my opinion, he is just another child to feed, and your living situation is not an example you would want your daughter to pattern their lives after when they are grown. Nor do you want your sons to become the kind of grown boy who will be a burden on a woman.

Ladies, I know sometimes it gets lonely in your homes and you desire the company of a man. Please believe me, I have been there and done that, and yes, it gets lonely sometimes a lot, but I will wait until Jesus gives me to the right man.

Women we have to allow Jesus to help us put our sexual desires, our feelings of loneliness, and our needs on wanting a man to take care of us on the back burner and busy ourselves by doing things that will make us better while we wait patiently for Jesus to send us our husbands. You must allow Jesus to place the right man in your path and then in your home.

Now I will tell you what I said I was going to tell you earlier in this chapter. I was in your place at one point in my life and had all five warning signs in one man in my home. Yes, honey, me and I promised myself that I would never, never ever do that to myself again, and I have not.

I did not just the next day say, "Get out," and just like magic, he was gone, and I was on the upswing. Oh no, I talked to him about it, and he tried to fight me to stay in my home, but I told him he had to go in thirty days.

That was time to allow him to find a job and move out, and if he had not done so, he still had to leave on that thirtieth day. I knew I was doing right and headed in the right direction because in talking to Jesus, crying and complaining about what was going on in my life, Jesus simply said to me, "You know what you should and should not be doing in your life, and you know what is pleasing in my sight."

Immediately, I began to start making drastic changes in my life. I felt a huge weight lift off my shoulders, and I breathed a sigh of relief and did not feel guilty about the changes I made in my life.

Some of you right now know exactly what I am talking about, and the rest of you need to get started on the major changes that need to take place in your lives. Yes, he moved out before the thirty days were up, but sadly, I must say it was just to the next woman who would take him in.

I realize some of you may stop reading this book after this chapter because you do not want to let go of that grown boy in your home. Let me assure you if you keep that grown boy in your home, you will never have the opportunity to experience the man that Jesus wants to give you.

Therefore, you decide—the grown boy you choose or the man Jesus has chosen to marry, love, cherish, and take care of you. Choose well, my sisters in Christ.

IF YOU HAVE MARRIED HIM

You may be saying to yourself, "OMG, yes, this is me. I married him. Oh my goodness, what do I do now? Is it too late?" I say to you no problem, calm down, and do not feel bad. Remember, love hides a multitude of sins, but Jesus is able to forgive us of them all.

I promise you, there is not a problem that Jesus cannot fix. You must first turn your marriage over to Jesus. Give Jesus complete control of the entire marriage, including you. Move out of the way and do whatever and everything Jesus tells you to do. He will have to grow this grown boy up before your very eyes, or He will tell you what to do if this grown boy refuses to grow up.

Remember, you married him, so he must have some qualities that you like and love, or you would not have married him. On the other hand, you probably were just blindsided by all of the five things you read in the preceding chapters. No matter the reason, you now carry his last name. You must pay very close attention to what you read next.

Sometimes what you want to do may get in the way, and it will not be what Jesus is saying for you to do. It is what you want to hear and do yourself. Please pay very close attention and be obedient to what Jesus will have you to do.

Pray, pray, and pray some more that you remove your desires, your will, and your wants out of the way, and let Jesus work on the grown boy that you have in your home. You cannot expect a grown boy to act or be a man if he has no idea on how to be something he knows nothing about. This is where Jesus comes in.

What better teacher to have than the Lord Himself; He will lead this grown boy in the right direction and grow him up for you or move him out of your way. In the meanwhile, do your part and just pray, listen, and be obedient to Jesus when He tells you to do something.

Jesus will also take the opportunity to work, straighten out, and input some things into you so you too maybe the wife for this man when he finishes with him. Look for changes in yourself to come as well, and be open to them. Do not say, "There is nothing wrong with me." If that is the case, how did you not recognize this grown boy and then marry him?

Okay, that is what I thought. You need help as well because if Jesus decides to move this grown boy out of your way, you need to make sure you do not choose another one in the future. So settle down, realize that there are lessons that you too must and will learn. Remember to stay out of Jesus's way and let him work on the grown boy and you.

HE IS NOT FOR YOU

Where do I start? Ah, here is a good place. Let us start with the truth. Some women already know that the man they are with is not the man for them. For whatever reason you have told yourself or convinced yourself that you are with the right person is beyond me.

Women, it is time to wake up and stop fooling yourself because you know it is a lie. You know in your heart of hearts that he is not right for you. You say he has a good job. So what? It is his. He has a nice house and a car; it is his. He is fun to be around, so is a puppy.

These are some of the dumbest reasons and the wrong reasons to be with a man, and yet women do it all the time. Just because he has those things does not necessarily make him a good man, and you know it.

With determination and hard work, you can have everything he has. If you need to further your education to land yourself a great job so you can have your own money, buy your own nice house and car and have your own fun, then do it.

Sometimes, women chase men for the dumbest reasons. I am here to tell you that a woman has no business chasing a man or looking for a man. Proverbs 18:22 says, "He who findeth a wife findeth a good thing and obtaineth favor of the Lord." This scripture does not say, "She who goes out and gets her own husband or chase a man down." It clearly states he will come find you.

Let me say that again; it clearly states he will come find you. So many women have a problem with that scripture because it requires them to wait, and most of you are very impatient when it comes to waiting on God to give you to the man he has created just for you.

So you go out, pick the man you want (not the one God wants to give you to), and land yourselves in some of the most messed-up situations, not to mention the situations that have left you feeling the way you do right now.

Some situations are the reason you are reading this book. Some of you have created the hell you are in, and the rest of you have allowed a grown boy, or the decision you made because you wanted a man so bad landed you where we are in life.

Ladies, you must take a few steps back and wait on God for the man He wants to put in your life. Just face it, some of you are in situations you want to be out of, but you feel like you cannot get out. If you are single and not married to the situation you are in, honey, it is simple.

Just walk away, and thank God you realized he was not right for you. If you are married and you realize you chose wrong, it is time to pray and seek counsel from God on how to handle your situation. It is time to wake up from the foolishness and tell yourself the truth that the man you chose just may not be the one for you.

Oh and by the way, telling or asking Jesus to bless the mess you created is not going to work. You see, Jesus cannot bless that which He has cursed. Let me explain the previous sentence.

You see, if you chose the man you are with, then you are already out of the order of life. God gave Eve to Adam; she did not go out and find him. You may have also chosen the man you are with because he has money and material things.

Well, you are wrong and once again out of order. Allow me to share some knowledge with you. A man's body is strong for a reason. God made him that way because he has to go to work, provide, and take care of his family. The reason a man is supposed to have a job, house, and car is because when God gives him one of His daughters, he is to take up where God left off and take good care of her just as God was doing while it was just her and God.

You see, some of you women do not even know why you chase a man for the things he has. You chase him because the things he has provide security for you, just as God had given that responsibility to Adam to take care of Eve.

Read that whole paragraph again. Let it marinate for a while in your brain. There is no need in making your life and the man's life you are with miserable just because he has nice things.

You know this man is not for you, but you will stick it out so you will not have to work or because you love the plush life he affords you, but at what cost? What are you willing to take from or off this man because of the plush or lavish life he is able to give you? Is it a beating? Or maybe not a beating, just a slap or two here and there? Or being talked down to, or being cheated on?

What is that lifestyle he provides for you worth? Just as you sold yourself to him because of what he has, you relinquished yourself and your rights to an opinion or anything to him because of what he has. There is another woman out there, willing to do the same thing as you did, and if she is prettier than you, guess what? Yes, the next seller of goods will replace you.

I pray that after reading this chapter, you will start thinking about your life and realizing how important life really is and how your happiness and peace of mind are not worth material things. Just remember, Jesus cannot and will not make a mistake in the man that He has chosen for you. Trust Jesus, be patient, and wait on Him to give you to the man that He wants to give you to.

Life can be just as good and even better with the right man in your life who loves you and wants to give you things because he loves you without you having to sacrifice anything just to be with him. He will be with you and love you, and this is the will of God for you.

NO CALLS

W here do I began on this subject? Oh, right here: Stop it, stop it, stop it. Ladies, if the man you were with is no longer in your life, with you or around you, tell me something—why are you still calling him and he is not calling you? Not only is he not calling you, he is not even answering your calls and he has blocked you.

If he has blocked you, do not call him from someone else's phone because he will also block that number and every number you try to use to call him. Leave that man alone. So tell me again why you are still calling this man.

I know why. You hope he will come to his senses and come back to you. Really, did you ever stop to think that maybe God has moved him out the way so someone better can come along? On the other hand, the plain truth is he was not the one for you. If he was the one for you and you messed up the relationship by what you did, then accept your responsibility.

The fact is he is gone and no longer wants to be with you. Move on and leave that man alone. I am more than sure he still knows and probably has your number, and if he should decide to call you, he knows where he can find you, but in the meanwhile, leave that man alone.

If he has moved on in life and is now with someone else, leave that man alone. If you wanted your cake and you wanted to eat it too and you lost the best man you ever had, move on because he has, and leave that man alone. None of your tricks or playing games will get him to come back to you, and I will tell you why. It is because he no longer wants to be with you, so leave that man alone.

Some of you women right now have restraining orders on you for bothering that man, and he has moved on. You should be ashamed of yourself for having to take it that far. Face it, move on, and leave that man alone.

Do not call, text, e-mail, Facebook, Instagram, send up a smoke signal, or do anything to him. Just leave that man alone. If you give him room, he may call or come back one day, and if not, then move on and do what? Yes, say it with me: leave that man alone.

VERBAL ABUSE

66 "Sticks and stones will break my bones but words will never hurt me" is the biggest lie on the face of the planet. Words do hurt, and they cut to the marrow while reverberating in your head.

I want to make this chapter especially clear. Oftentimes, women like to make excuses as to why this happen. Any name said to you in an intentional, hurtful, derogatory manner in which you were not born with is verbal abuse.

Any name describing your body or body parts in an intentional, hurtful, derogatory manner that hurts your feelings or make you feel humiliated or embarrassed is verbal abuse. You should not accept this abusive behavior. We all have flaws or something about our body that we would like to change.

I have heard men say they are motivating or trying to help the woman change by saying these mean and hurtful things. Make no mistake about it; this behavior is not motivating you, nor is it encouraging you to change or seek help for what someone else thinks is a flaw or problem you have.

Look at the individual from whom your verbal abuse is coming from, and see the flaws they have and feel better about yourself. Remember, something is seriously wrong with people who will put another person down.

Generally, these people have feelings of low self-esteem themselves and are having their own issues within themselves. Misery they say does love company, but do not allow anyone to invite you to that party. Allow them to pull that wagon on their own, and if you can encourage them to stop, the verbal abuse and seek help for what is wrong with them please do so.

Now it is time for some truth. Some of you are overweight and you know it, and I heard some women say, "If he does not like what he sees, he can close his eyes," and this is true. Let us get real for a moment being overweight is not healthy for anyone but a woman will accept an overweight man quicker than a man will accept an overweight woman.

I say that because women see the inside of a person and that is who we love. Most men are visual creatures, and they look at the outside package and make their decision from there. Therefore, whatever flaws you know you have, and you want to fix them or work on fixing them for yourself then do so but do not fix anything because someone else has a problem with it.

After all, you must love you first before someone else can love you. Remember verbal abuse is real and very wrong. Do not allow another individual to put you down or take away your self-esteem. So love yourself, and do not except verbal abuse from anyone.

IF HE HITS YOU

Now here is a touchy subject but nonetheless real. There is no reason, no excuse, and no explanation as to why a man should hit a woman. Love is what love does, and love does not hurt that which it loves. Am I right or am I right? He will say he is sorry and it will never happen again, but it will, and in fact, it should not have happened in the first place. He might even say, "Look what you made me do."

I do not think you took his hand, fist, foot, or whatever body part he used to hit, kick, punch, or strike you with and placed it on your body. He did that all by himself. So it was not, is not, nor will it ever be your fault that he cannot control his temper or anger and he takes it out on you. Now, let us talk about me.

Any man that has inappropriately put his hands on me—and there were three or four that did—he either got his throat cut or he was stabbed. I loved them, but I did not play that putting your hands on me stuff. I was not a punching bag, slapping stick, or a kickstand, and I made sure they knew it and would remember it for the rest of their life.

It caught me off guard when they slapped, pushed, or hit me, and it caught them off guard when I cut their throat or stabbed them. I know not every woman out there is strong like me, but there are some out there, and I am telling you to stand up for yourself by any means necessary.

Now I am not suggesting violence or that you should stand up for yourself in the manner in which I did, but I am saying to you stand up for yourself. If you do not think you can do this for yourself, that is what the police department is for; call the police.

Hot grits or grease while he is sleeping will get any man's attention and may even stop his violent behavior. Violence is not the way, but you must protect and stand up for yourself. Please pray and ask Jesus to deliver you from this type of relationship because it is not healthy at all.

Do not fool yourself and say, "I cannot make it without him because he pays the bills." It is okay to be afraid, but you must remove yourself from this situation. If you have children in this type of a situation, this is an even better reason to move from this situation.

Ask yourself how long it will be before he starts abusing the children because it happens every day, and do not dare say he will never do that. Some of you have said that, and some of you just said he is already abusing the children; this is why you must remove yourself and your children from this situation as fast as possible.

Physical abuse is wrong, and you should not tolerate abuse of any kind. There are men who will love you the way Jesus loves you and will not hurt you. If you are in a violent relationship and cannot stand up for yourself, run away when the opportunity presents itself, and I pray you will find a safe haven.

If you are in this type of relationship and are strong enough to leave, please do so. Get help from family, friends, and your church if you can, but leave immediately. As a little girl, you did not plan your life this way, so why live this way? Run and run fast from this situation. My prayers are with you.

IF HE CHEATS

What can I say about this subject? A cheater cheats because he is a cheater or unless you caused this action. I will explain the latter part of the previous sentence later. Under no circumstance should we except or tolerate this behavior. It is a self-indulging, self-gratifying, and disrespectful behavior.

It does not matter what reason you tell yourself or you allow him to tell you, he cheated and it is wrong. It was all about him, for him, and I am sure if you did not catch him or find out about it, he would have kept it to himself. If you allow this behavior to reoccur—and in most cases, it will reoccur—you surely will regret it. Cheating is like a snowball going downhill fast and picking up momentum as it rolls.

If this has happened one time and you believe he truly is sorry for his actions, and you both had counseling and you can forgive him, please do so and move on. When I say move on, I mean move on and not hang on to it to bring it back up during an argument or try to use it as an advantage point during your relationship. Rarely will cheating happen one time, but there are instances where it has happened.

Now, we must admit and tell the truth. There are some dirty low-down scoundrels out here who will cheat and lie about it and then tell you that you made him do it. Sugar, be real with yourself and tell the truth.

You know what you have at home, and if you like it, then something is wrong. Some of you women know you have the devil in pants under your roofs. You lie to your-selves and say he will change, it is just a phase, or he will stop. Caterpillars go through a phase, babies go through a phase, but a grown man does not go through a phase when he cheats.

He has plenty of time to stop and think about what he is doing before he inserts his penis inside a vagina that is not yours. Ladies, do not be fooled. He is not having sex because of a phase; he is having sex as his choice. Why should his dumb choices determine your life and hurt your feelings and your heart?

If this is your man and you are not married to him, honey, kick his lying, cheating, good-for-nothing butt to the curb and don't look back. You do not deserve that, and

I promise you there is a man out here looking for a good woman he can love and be faithful to.

Now if you are married to this grown boy, your situation is different. Some women are strong and have the means and a great support system where they too can walk away and kick his lying, cheating, good-for-nothing butt to the curb.

However, some women out here do not have any of the above-mentioned support systems and may feel as if though they are trapped in their present situation. I understand he may provide the only income in the house or he may rule with an iron fist.

Ladies, you are not trapped in your present situation. Here is your way out: prayer, Jesus, your church family (if you have one), and just someone God may send to help you will be a way out, and you will be free of your situation. This all depends on if you want to be free.

Now to explain the latter part of the first sentence I made in the first paragraph of this chapter. Some women like to use sex as a weapon in their homes. Unless the man does whatever the woman says, he gets no sex.

Some of you women have put your husbands on a one or two-day-a-week schedule, meaning they can only have sex with you on Saturday, Thursday, Wednesday, or

Monday. This type of behavior is foolish, reckless, and stupid. You will cause a man to go out and cheat.

If you have done this and started a cycle of cheating in your home because of your action, you deserve exactly what you got. I am sure by now some of you are sorry for your behavior and want the behavior that you created in your mate to stop. Well, you will not get off so easy. Because you created the monster (meaning the cheating), now you have to destroy the beast.

Prayer, Jesus, and counseling can help you if it is not too late. If it is too late, then you not only destroyed your home, but only the Lord knows how many more other homes as well. What do I mean by other homes?

If you are married and you caused him to go cheat because of your behavior holding sex as a weapon, when he cheats, that is adultery, and the person he is cheating with is committing either adultery or fornication, and therefore, two homes are being destroyed.

In God's eyes, both people are wrong, the adulterer and the fornicator. So now, you have destroyed two homes, but both people had a choice to make so you get 60 percent of the blame because you started it, and they get 20 percent each for the decision they made.

Ladies, whatever the scenario, cheating must end. Do not be gullible, foolish, naive or ignore about what you know to be happening. A woman's intuition tells her what is going on. Believe it, trust it, and ask God to reveal the truth if you do not know or suspect something is going on. Do not accuse him of cheating without having concrete evidence, real facts, or truth, and you can move on from there.

If you started the behavior of cheating because of your actions, ask for forgiveness from Jesus first and then from your husband, and I hope and pray that things will work out for you. Do not allow a man to lie to you, hurt you, or cheat on you any longer. Girl, wake up.

IF YOU CHEAT

I am going to keep telling the truth, so I must say this as well. Just as there are some trifling men in this world, we also know that there are some trifling women as well. We all have said it: "How in the world did her low-down butt get such a good man? She does not treat him right, and she does not deserve him." Yes, I know it is mind-blowing, but these things do happen.

Nevertheless, women, let me say this: I am writing a book for the men as well that will wake them up too. Women like this will not be in their relationships long because you can kick a dog long enough, and it will bite you or run away.

Men who find themselves being misled and duped by women like this will have their eyes opened, and it will be curtains for this type of woman as well.

If you are one of these women that I am talking about in this chapter, my advice to you is to stop your behavior at once and appreciate the good man that you have. It will not be long before one day either something he will read or someone he will meet will open his eyes to what it is like to be with a kindhearted and loving woman.

Someone who will show him love and respect and will appreciate the things he does for her—when he finds such a woman (please believe me when I tell you he is looking), this will be the end of your good life as you know it. You do not have to believe me. Just keep doing what you're doing, and you will soon discover that I was telling the truth.

If you do not know how to stop and change your behavior and you wish to, ask Jesus for help on changing and correcting your behavior. Search out groups and counseling that will help you to change your behavior. You are grown and you know that cheating is wrong, and it does not matter what the reason is for your cheating, it must stop.

Allow Jesus to teach you to start appreciating the good man that you have in your life because there are plenty women in the world looking, wishing, waiting, and wanting a good man.

SHACKING UP

What can I say about this? Oh, I know! It is wrong. Even in the Garden of Eden, Adam had to wait for God to make a mate for him, and God gave him Eve. I said that to say this, some of you refuse to be alone and will allow any man, even the wrong man, to move into your home or you move into his just to keep from being lonely.

Ladies, is it really that deep for you? Sometimes, women, God wants you to be alone with Him so He can get you ready for the man He wants to put in your life. However, you will not wait on God; you just allow any Tom, Dick, and Harry in your hearts, lives, and houses just to keep from being lonely. This is a big mistake.

Now some of you have gotten yourselves into some messed-up situations and relationships because you did not want to be alone. Go ahead; admit it; you know I am telling the truth. Now you want that man out your house so bad, you could bite nails, but you let him in, and now it is going to take an act of congress to get him out.

After you let him in, now you are grumbling, complaining, fussing at, and arguing with him all the time, and now you are so miserable and you now wish you had stayed alone or lonely. Well, allow me to help you solve your problem by saying this: he must go. While you continue to shack up with him, he is blocking blessings that God wants to give you.

Even worse, some of you are raising a child or children in this messed-up situation. Ask yourself what you are teaching your child or children about how you are living. This is not the type of behavior you would want your sons and daughters to accept and think is okay. I can tell you this is not what you want to teach your sons or daughters.

Now, let me tell you one of my personal stories. I allowed a grown boy to move in my house because I loved him and I was lonely. I thought it could not hurt anything and I would have some company. Well, let me tell you that this was the worst thing I could have ever done in my life.

This man tried to cause a rift between my children and me. He was jealous of the attention I gave my children. He tried to take over my household and tried to tell my children and me what we should and should not be doing.

We argued all the time until finally I said, "Get out." I had enough, and no one, especially no man, will ever come between my children and me. As soon as I put him out of my house, blessings started to pour in from everywhere.

Now I did not say you would not receive blessings, but you are not receiving all the blessings you could be receiving if you only did things the way that God said to do them. If he loves you that much, then he should marry you and make an honest woman out of you.

For those of you that say I am just being old-fashioned, you bet your sweet potato I am, and old-fashioned leads to forty, fifty, and sixty-year marriages. Shacking only leaves a mess of you and your child or children because when you break up with the man, so does your child or children, and they do not deserve to be hurt because of your insecurities. It also leads you to reading a book entitled *Girl, Wake Up*.

If you are afraid to be alone and tired of being lonely, may I suggest that you go buy yourself a pet. It is low-maintenance and will love you unconditionally. You will not have to argue with it, and it will not block any of your blessings. You are being manipulated by your feelings, and you should control them and not let them control or dictate your life.

Time is precious and does not need to be wasted. You cannot get that back once it is gone. Use it wisely, marry, or get off the pot. No more shacking.

DO NOT ALLOW A MAN TO WASTE YOUR TIME

Some of you are in marriages and relationships that you know are going nowhere. For the women who are in dead-end relationships, here is my advice to you: Get out. How many years have you been hanging around that dead relationship, waiting on him to pop the question? More than one year is one year to long.

Face it; this man knew six months into the relationship if he wanted to marry you or not. Now it is years later and probably some children also, and you are still allowing him to tell you he will one day marry you while he continues to get the milk free. All the cooking, cleaning, and sex you are giving him with no commitment—he is satisfied and set for life in hog's heaven, so why should he marry you? He has it all, and you have a false hope and an empty promise of marriage.

Oh and by the way, if you have to give him an ultimatum to marry you, sugar, believe me when I say he does not want to marry you, okay? If you have to give hints and pull pranks to get him to marry you, then he is not the one for you, and he does not want to marry you; please believe me.

Five men have proposed to me during my lifetime, and it did not take any one of those men longer than a year to ask me. I said no, but that story is for another book. A man knows whether he wants to marry you when he enters into a relationship with you.

You better not dare let him tell you he does not know because yes, he does. Stop trying to make him marry you and move on. If you have to make him marry you, honey, he does not want to marry you.

You are wasting valuable time and cutting yourself off from the one who so desperately wants to meet you and be with you and marry you. So hurry up and move on. He is out there and wondering where you are. Free yourself so he can find you.

The advice I just gave is for women who are single and not married to the man. Now, if you are in a dead marriage, this is a different situation. You must go to God and seek His counsel and wisdom on what to do in your situation.

Marriage is a very delicate situation and something I do not take lightly. If God joined you together, He can save your marriage. I did say, "If God joined you together," because there are many marriages out there that God did not join together. Just because the preacher said, "What God has joined together let no man put asunder," does not mean that God joined you together.

Those words are just part of the marriage vows. I said that to say this. Some people joined themselves together because she or he has money, looks, and material things or just because they are tired of being alone and lonely.

Whatever the reason you joined yourselves together, if it is for reasons other than love, you still must seek counsel from God, for He knows all. It does not matter how you ended up in a dead marriage. You are there, and you must not allow a man to waste your time. Time is the one thing that once it is gone, you will never get it back.

When you finish reading this chapter, take a few moments, sit in silence, and talk to God. Pray about your situation, ask for guidance, and follow the advice God gives you. He will never lead you in the wrong direction, and it may be difficult to do whatever He tells you to do, but remember, God knows what is best for you and He wants only the best for you. Allow Him to give you His best.

Things just may work out the way you want them to. Just remember whatever Jesus says to do is the best thing to do for the both of you. Most importantly, please remember: do not allow a man to waste your time.

DID HE CHOOSE WRONG?

I am sure there are some men out here who are kicking themselves in the butt because they are in a relationship or married to some of you. I do not care if you got mad at my prior sentence; you have already bought the book, so keep reading. Ladies, some of you know you act as if though Satan is your father. You are mean to your man, you talk down to him, you do not respect or appreciate him, and you know he is a good man.

He is probably thinking and saying to himself, "What have I gotten myself into and how can I get out of it?" Maybe he is thinking and hoping you will change. We all know only Jesus, along with the teaching and guiding of the Holy Spirit, can change a person, and that is only if that person wants to change.

Let me give you a few facts and some advice. The number of good available men is diminishing fast. I have heard it said that it was ten women to every one man. Now let us figure in the number of men that are going to jail or prison daily, so now the ratio of females to males goes up dramatically.

Therefore, when someone says it is hard to find a good man, it really is, but remember, it is not for a woman to look for a man. It is his job to come find you. Now it is okay for you to put yourself in places to be found, but do not go hunting.

Now, here is my advice to you: stop acting like a donkey's rear end, and treat the good man that you have with respect and dignity. When he decides that he is sick and tired of the way you are treating him, he will leave you, and that is a fact. You may choose to ignore what you just read, but I guarantee you that when it comes true, you will remember what you read in this book.

Let us not forget there are plenty of good women out here waiting for a good man to come find them, and women, if you are patient, Jesus will lead a good man right to you. For the women who are treating a good man bad, let me give you some warning signs that he is thinking, considering, and planning to leave you.

He is quiet now and no longer wants to talk to you anymore. He stays out or comes home later and later. You think it is another woman, but the truth is he no longer wants to be around you. The lovemaking has stopped, and he sleeps with his back toward you now, and you are too stupid to care.

Here is the biggest sign of all: he no longer argues with you anymore. He agrees and moves on. Do not make the mistake of thinking you have won the argument, and you probably think you did. No, honey, he does not argue with you anymore because he is planning to leave you.

Now if you should chose to continue in your present behavior, then enjoy the results, which will be the end of your relationship as you know it. Oh, and the new woman that now has your ex—he and she are in love, and he is treating her the way he wanted to treat you, but your behavior would not allow him to treat you in such a manner.

If you want to change, ask Jesus to help you change so you will not let a good man slip away because once he is gone—I can guarantee you—you will not find anyone else who will put up with your behavior.

WHEN IT HURTS

If you are reading this book, I know one thing for sure. At some point in your life, a grown boy has hurt you. I am sure that every woman has suffered some hurt in her life that she feels she just cannot get over or thinks she has gotten over but still holds it in the back of her mind or heart. I pray this chapter and this book will free you. You are not free, nor are you healed if you still have feelings or thoughts about the hurt just hanging around out there in your life.

How you have either handled or not handled it has lead you to reading this book for either guidance, help, healing, self-discovery, or whatever the reason God has lead you to read this book. I can guarantee you that there is something in here that can do all the above and more with the help of Jesus.

You must be willing to admit the hurt, guilt, anger, shame, or whatever it is that you are holding on to that will not allow you to heal, and then turn it over to Jesus so that the healing process can began. You cannot fully love others until you first love yourself completely. You cannot make others happy until you are completely happy from within.

So many times women look for a man to make them happy or try to find happiness in things or sex even. If you look for a man, money, or things to make you happy when this man, the money, or these things are no longer in your life, there goes your happiness.

Start today; determine today that you will be the reason you are happy and that you will no longer look for others or things to make you happy. Healing always start from the inside, and only Jesus knows you so intimately inside that He and He alone can heal you completely and restore you unto your oneness with Him and then with yourself.

Go get a pen and paper, and write down all your past and present hurts. Now ask God to reveal to you hidden things that are hurting you as well. You must first have all the hurt exposed to yourself, and this will allow your healing process to begin. This process will hurt and make you angry, and you will shed many, many, many tears, but that is the healing process.

Go through this process, scream, shout, cry, and then began to heal. The second step to healing is forgiveness. You must forgive the person or people who have hurt you and left you with the hurt even if they have gone to the grave. Forgiveness will free you of all your hurts and pain.

This process will not take overnight to do, so take it one step at a time, and allow Jesus to lead you down the road to a healthier, happier, and more fulfilled life. If healing is what you seek, healing is what you will not only find but also receive.

HOW IS YOUR ATTITUDE?

Many women are still single, and some cannot keep a man if he tied himself to her. Some women remain single or in bad relationships because of their bad attitudes. Yes, I said your bad attitude. We all know some woman who has a bad or stank attitude, and if you do not know a woman like that, then you are that woman.

The women with the attitudes just said, "I do not have an attitude." Honey, the first step to recovery is to admit that you do have a problem. Let me tell you this: there is nothing cute about having a bad attitude and being proud of it. I used to be that way until I realized it was getting me nowhere with people or in life. I had an attitude, and the more people told me I had an attitude, the more I had an attitude.

Until one day I had to realize that my attitude was not just hurting me, it was also hurting my children. What I mean by this is my attitude was preventing me from getting jobs I wanted because people could see my stubbornness could not be changed, and that overshadowed my great qualities.

Some of you are the same way right now. You have great qualities and attributes that can help a company or person, but because your attitude speaks louder than your qualities, you do not get the job, and the man you want decides he just does not want to be around or be bothered with your attitude.

So I had to ask Jesus to help me to change my attitude and change it fast. No matter how much it hurt me to do this, this was necessary, not only for my life to be better but so that I could give my children a better life. I strongly suggest those of you who have an attitude problem (every woman with an attitude problem knows she has one) and are willing to change, please ask Jesus for help right now. I mean it. Stop reading right now and say, "Jesus, I know I have an attitude problem, and I see how it is affecting my life in a negative way.

I want to change and do not know how to change, so please, I am asking you to help me to change my attitude so that I may begin to live a more productive and healthier life."

Now, if you do not have children to change for, change because you know you need to, and I pray you want to because you can only go up from where you are. Where you are right now, I am sure, is not such a happy place, and I am sure you would not want to spend the rest of your life unhappy, and this is why you are reading this book.

Whatever your reason or desire is to change—it is the best reason to start the change in your attitude. You are on the right track, and you and the world will be so happy when you begin to change. You and your attitude will reach new heights in altitude, and life will be sweeter for you. I guarantee it.

HOW ARE YOUR COMMUNICATION SKILLS?

We wish for, pray for, and would love to have this in a man, but the reality of it is this will never happen. Face it, women; the reality of the situation is a man will never be able to do this. "What is this?" you ask. Read your mind. Never in a million years will this happen. So tell me, women, why is it that you get so upset when your mate says, "Just tell me what you want because I cannot read your mind?"

The man is telling you the truth; he cannot read your mind. So give him a break, and stop trying to make the man take on the job as mind reader as well as provider. In as much as you are not going to like my next sentence, you have to read it and take heed to it. Stop making your life and his life difficult by throwing temper tantrums like a child and tell the man what you want.

Life can and will be sweeter for the both of you if you just spell it out and stop beating that bush and him to death. You cannot read minds, and you think of yourself as the being with more intelligence, so why should you hold him accountable for not being able to do something that you cannot do?

Think about the former sentence for a minute. You know I am right. In short, spell it out, say it, and give the man a break. If he can relax and not be a mind reader, he just might surprise you and read your action, which will be your thoughts.

There is nothing wrong with a hint or two every now and then. Besides, we are talking about a man here; the more hints, the better. Men work or think according to a woman's actions and also off what you say, so be careful of the vibe you are putting out, and watch what you say because he just may get confused and you cannot blame him.

Be obvious and direct at the same time without being obvious and direct if you can. You are a woman, so I know you can do this. Maybe this way, you will stop confusing the poor fellow. So remember to work on your own communication skills before you try to improve on someone else's skills.

Pray and always ask Jesus for help to make your relationship skills and communications skills better between the two of you, and life will be smoother, better, and less volatile for the both of you.

HELP YOUR MATE

There are some men out there who work an eight, ten, or twelve-hour shift job and still have to come home, cook, and clean. Some have to take care of children as well while some of you laaazy, sorry, trifling, no-account women (you know who you are) who do nothing all day but sit around the house.

This is the worst kind of woman—a lazy, sorry woman who will not help her man when she knows he is doing all he can to support and provide for the family. To you I say, "You should be ashamed of yourself." We should kick you out the girls' club; we should pull your card because you do not deserve it.

There are so many women looking and waiting for a good man. You seem to have ended up with one, and you do not appreciate or deserve him at all. You should be ashamed, and I only pray that you come to your senses and help that man or that he comes to his senses and leave you. Yes, I said, "Leave you," because no one should be subjected to that type of torture.

A lazy woman is a disgrace to real women, and you should be a shamed if this is you. I strongly suggest you change your ways before you have a rude awakening, such as finding yourself alone again. I do not care if you just got mad at me for calling you out. I called you out so that you will have your eyes opened and to show you all you have to lose.

You should seek counseling and get help so you can figure out and understand why you are lazy and why you refuse to help a good man. Surely, no one is that lazy and inconsiderate of someone else's feelings. In this economy, it takes two people to make a living. If the man is working enough where his income will support the household, consider yourself blessed.

So get up off your butt and take care of that man like he is going to work to take care of you. If one income is not enough, help that man. Go get a part-time or full-time job. Do not just sit around the house doing nothing and watch that man work himself to death for you. I understand that sometimes there can be a chemical imbalance in the brain that will leave a person feeling depressed, but there is medication and help for that.

I am not talking to you. I am talking to that woman who is just flat out lazy and refuses to do anything to help her man. If you keep not appreciating him, believe me, some woman will catch his eye, and you will find yourself left out in the cold.

ARE YOU A HEALED WOMAN?

Ladies, it is time to face the truth about yourself and answer this question: Are you a healed woman? You know whether you are or if you are not a healed woman. You pray, cry, and ask God for a man or a husband. Allow me to interject some truth into your situation.

If God were to put that man in some of your lives, he would run and run fast away from you. "Why I say this?" you may ask. I say this because most women are such an emotional wreck because of what some grown boy has done to them or because of some of the things they have allowed themselves to get mixed up in.

Some of you are waiting on a man to come along and help you straighten out the mess you have gotten or allowed yourselves to get in. When and if this man does come along, you will put all your baggage on him and say,

"Fix this mess," and it will be too much for him to bear, so he will run.

He may try to help you in the beginning, but he will soon realize that trying to help you will become so overwhelming; it will be like a sponge trying to soak up the ocean. It will not happen. He will realize he is out of his league and that your baggage is too much for him to handle.

Therefore, he will slowly fade himself out of your life, or he will suddenly move himself fast out of your life. Either way he does it, he will be gone.

If you are waiting on a man to come along and help with the hurts, disappointments, shame, regrets, or whatever you have going on in your life, this means it is too much for you to bear alone as well.

Therefore, what makes you think one single man can bear all your pain and problems and you at the same time? Stop praying for a man and start praying for Jesus to heal you from the inside out. Jesus is the only man who can, who will, and who wants to bear all of your hurts, pains, and disappointments and the only one who can heal you as well.

Face it, women; you must stop depending on a man to heal or help you heal. That is Jesus's job because no one knows you better than He does. Only Jesus loves you unconditionally, and it does not matter what type of emotional damage you have allowed yourselves to get into. He wants to heal and restore you completely.

Once Jesus has healed you, you will begin to feel better about yourself, and you will be ready to get into that relationship with the right man. You will be healthy, healed, and ready to take on the world with a new perspective and a new view about yourself and your life.

ARE YOU A GOOD WOMAN?

Here is some reality for you. There are some women out here who are trifling, conniving and laaazy. They often either think or ask themselves this question: Why can I not keep a man or why do I not have a man? Now some of us can answer that question for them, and we'll be glad to give them an answer that they might not like.

I will give you my answer and tell you why I know you do not have or cannot keep a man. It is because of the way you are scheming and plotting to get a man. Oh yes, there are women in this world who will scheme and plot just to get a man. These women will buy fake pregnancy tests (yes, I said *fake pregnancy test*).

There are fake positive pregnancy tests for sale online, and some women buy these tests and use them to trick the man to get him to stay with them by showing him one of these fake tests. Now if I am not mistaken, I think this fake pregnancy game has been around for years, and I have yet to see a baby keep a man.

Now if you do trick him into getting you pregnant just to keep him, he may hang around for a while, but once and if he finds out what you did was just a trick to either get him or keep him, well, I am sure the end result will not work out in your favor. Not to mention the poor child you have brought into your mess.

Some of these women will threaten to have an abortion unless the man stay with them and they know they are not pregnant, and some will threaten him to stay if they are pregnant.

I have heard about women using the urine of a pregnant woman or friend so they can take a test in front of their boyfriend to show him they are pregnant. There are all kinds of crazy ways to trap a man, and this is ridiculous. This is what I mean by scheming and plotting.

Ladies, listen. If you have to trick him to get him or keep him, then he does not want you and you should move on. Why be with someone who does not want to be with you? If you have to trick, lie, or deceive him to get him, do you not realize you will have to keep doing that to keep him?

Now what man is worth all of that? Your lies and tricks will catch up with you one day; I promise you they will.

You will not get away with your lies and your tricks, and maybe you will for a little while, but when he finds out about your lying and your tricks (and he will find out), he will leave you. He will be gone, and all your lies and tricks would have been for nothing. You lose and you are back to square one, alone again.

Now here is what I mean about being trifling and conniving. The man works hard for his paycheck, brings it home, and gives it all to you because he trusts you to pay the bill and do right by him.

Noooooo, your trifling and conniving butt pays something on the bills and then goes to buy some shoes or clothing you have had your eyes on, and you don't tell him what you did. The next thing you know, you are behind in rent, mortgage, bills, and car note, not to mention groceries. Your trifling and conniving behavior has landed the two of you in a bind all because he trusted you to do the right thing with the money.

Now he is going to leave you, and you are begging, crying, and trying to get him to stay. Why should he stay with you? You were not honest with this man, and he trusted you. It is your fault deal with your trifling and conniving behavior. Own it because it is all you.

Now for the next scenario, you finally get a man and now you are treating him bad, or—here is my favorite—

you get a man and you act as if though he owes you the world because you chose him.

Some of you women out here have good men who go to work religiously to bring home the bacon, and you will not even make sure the house is clean or the man has a good home-cooked meal when he gets home. You are tri-fling and lazy and do not deserve a good man or any man.

I heard you say, "Well, I got him." Yes, you may have him, but you will not have him for long. There is a woman out there praying for a good man who she can treat like a king because he gets up, goes to work, pays the bills, and treats her like a queen. I guarantee you, she will end up with him.

A man will tolerate your foolishness but only for so long, so you better straighten up and fly right, or he will be gone. I can promise you that. I am not here to dog you women, but I am here to call a spade a spade and to let you know certain behaviors that are not acceptable and must be changed.

If the man is doing right by you, treating you and your children right—that is if you have children—and the bills are paid, and you do not have to work, treat that man with all the respect he is due because he has earned it. It is your duty to keep the house clean, make sure his clothes are clean, make sure he has a good home-cooked meal, and I do not mean pizza.

If you do not know how to cook, go to the thrift store and buy some cookbooks. They are ninety-nine cents. Ask your mom, your friends, his mom, the dog, or cat—I do not care who you ask—just ask someone to teach you how to cook or follow a recipe book.

Now that you know you need to change and you are willing to change these behaviors, Jesus is willing, waiting, and wanting to help you. He loves you too much to leave you in the condition or shape that you are currently in. Jesus desires to help you not just for a man; he desires to help you change so you can become a better you.

THE NATURAL YOU

I see it every day—women piling on tons of makeup to cover up the natural skin they were born with. It sickens me to see women not feel confident in their natural skin. I know sometimes life can and will leave you with physical scars, and sometimes you want to cover them up, but when the makeup is off, do you love who you see in the mirror?

Society, television, men, and even some women have made women feel insignificant, less than worthy, and worst of all, left them with low self-esteem. For women to turn on each other in this manner is a travesty and a shame. You should not allow anyone or anything to define who you are, and you certainly should not put on makeup to cover up who you are.

I believe that if women would take the money that they spend on makeup and put it into a savings account, they would have a lot of money by Christmas and could really buy themselves something they really need or want.

How much more money would you have for bills, gas, groceries, and maybe an extra pair of shoes if you did not wear makeup. The face you put on is not the face you were born with.

We have all seen a woman who either was burned or has vitiligo in the face, and yet these women are married and in relationships because the man loves them and because they love themselves. They go through life with no makeup on, and they love who they see in the mirror.

On the other hand, we have women piling on makeup, covering up their natural skin to look lighter, have smoother skin, or just trying to look younger. Go right now to a mirror, look at yourself without the makeup on, and really look at yourself. Start loving who you are and who you see in the mirror.

Fall in love with her all over again, and I promise you that the world will love you when you love yourself. Many men have told me that they do not like all that makeup, false boobies, false eyelashes, and fake hair, and some women do all this to get their attention.

Some of you women just found out why the man you are looking at will not give you the time of day. Maybe it is because he cannot see who you really are because the real you is hiding under the makeup and everything else false that you had to buy. I know it will be a transition, and you will not go from makeup to wearing no makeup overnight, although some of you will.

Start with less makeup until you start to feel confident in yourself. Then progress to no makeup, and you will love yourself without the makeup because in the end, it is all about you anyway. You cannot hide guilt, shame, hurt, or anything else behind makeup.

Start dealing with your problems and the reasons as to why you wear the makeup or hide behind it, and who knows? You will probably find out that you did not need it in the first place. You will learn that you are beautiful just the way you are.

WHAT IS YOUR UNIFORM
SAYING ABOUT YOU?

A police officer wears a police officer uniform because he is a police officer. A firefighter wears a firefighter uniform because he is a firefighter. A nurse wears a nurse's uniform because she is a nurse. Do you see where I am going with this? Now let us talk about your uniform.

In other words, let us talk about the clothes on your back and in your closet. There are woman who walk the streets wearing shorts so short that their butt cheeks are hanging out, blouses so low-cut that their breasts are exposed, and clothing so tight that you can see their imagination. The world calls these women whores or prostitutes, so I guess it is safe to assume they are wearing a whore's uniform.

This is also true for the women who work for escort services while trading sex for money. Wait a minute. There are women out here who dress like that, and they are not on a corner. You see them in your grocery stores, malls, and some even in the church—yes, I said the church.

What does your clothes and the way you dress say to people? Do your clothes say, "I am educated, smart, classy, intelligent, and respectful," or do they say the opposite? Sometimes some women wonder why it is that a certain man will not speak to them or give them the time of day.

When a man looks at a woman, he has already made up in his mind who and what you are to him. If you are dressed like a one nightstand, then a grown boy will treat you as a one nightstand. A man will never treat a woman inappropriately because a man knows how to treat a woman if you conduct yourself and dress as a woman.

Ladies, it really is important how you dress because your clothing says so much about you. Some of you might say, "I do not care what a man thinks about how I dress, I dress how I want to dress." This is part of the reason as to why you are still alone and single, along with that nasty attitude of yours.

You do not have to care, but I guarantee you that a real man does care about how you dress because if he takes you out, you will be a reflection of him. Tight shorts, skirts, dresses or see-through dresses, blouses, and skirts have no place in church. Are you going to commune with God or get the attention of the men? The men may look, but you had also better know they are talking about you as well.

Women, if you are single and dressing like this, think about the message you are sending to men and look at the responses you are receiving. If he wants to take you out to dinner and then take you to the bedroom, what did your clothing say to him? Did they say, "I am easy" or did they say, "Do not even think about it?"

If you are married and wear clothing such as this out the house, shame on you and your husband for allowing you to come out the house looking like a streetwalker. Your body is for your husband's eyes only and not for other men to look and see through your clothes what is meant only for your husband. A real man will not have his wife leave the house in such a manner, but a grown boy will not care.

Ladies, let us be real. We all probably have at least five mirrors in our home, and we as women will look in all of them before we leave the house. So when you are out in public and you hear someone say, "No, she did not wear that," "What in the world was she thinking?" or "Was her mirror broke at home when she looked in it?" do not get angry.

Remember, you looked in the mirror before you left your house and approved of what you were wearing. If a grown boy approaches you in a manner you do not like, remember you looked in the mirror before you left your house and approved of what you were wearing.

Men, when you hear other men talking about your wife and how they want to have sex with her, do not get upset. You saw what she was wearing before she left the house and you approved it. Ladies, do you see where I am going with this? The way you dress says a lot about who and what you are.

So, make sure before you leave your house that you are conveying to the public and to men what you really want to say through your uniform. Remember, less is more only in makeup, not your clothing.

WHAT IS YOUR WORTH

What do you think of yourself? If you could place a value on yourself, what would the value be? What would be your dollar amount? Some of you would say you have little value. I say you are wrong. You are worth the blood of Jesus Christ. He thought so much of you that He died for you to redeem you back to the Father.

In other words, you are priceless. Some of you would place a dollar amount on yourself for millions, if not billions, and that is great. Here is my question to some of you: Why do you cheapen your value by sleeping around with so many men that you have lost count, or why do you sleep with men for money?

Some of you sleep with men for your rent and utility bills. My question to you is "Why have you allowed a grown boy to depreciate you, your value, and your body?" Is it the grown boy's fault?

No, the blame is all yours. Whatever reason you gave to yourself for this type of behavior—it is not a good enough reason. I do understand some of you are upset with me right now for allowing you to see the truth of your situation. If this destructive behavior is in your past, asks Jesus for forgiveness, forgive yourself, and move on.

If this remains your destructive behavior and you are reading this chapter, it is time for a change permanently. You must see yourself as being worth the blood of Jesus because you were to Him and still are worth His blood and His life He gave for you.

A grown boy will treat you the way you allow him to treat you. I repeat: a grown boy will treat you the way you allow him to treat you. You are so valuable, and I pray that you can see that in yourself.

Ladies, I am sure we all know a woman who is displaying this type of destructive behavior. We must be the first to help each other. Talking about the person or ganging up on them is not helpful, so please stop tearing one another down and extend a hand.

As women, we all need love and affection. We want it, we crave it so much, and this is why some of you have found yourselves in precarious situations and relationships. Pray for guidance before you approach a woman in this situation.

Pray so that she will receive instruction and guidance from Jesus on how to change her life. Pray and ask the Holy Spirit for guidance on what to say to this woman, and you keep your opinion to yourself; speak only Gods' words to her.

You know what they say about opinions. If you do not know, I will tell you. They say people opinions are like a butt hole; everybody has one. Whatever reason a woman tells herself why she is reckless with her body—that is not a good reason; it is an excuse. If you are serious about changing and stopping this destructive behavior, throw out all the reasons and excuses you have, and start praying and looking for a way out.

Jesus can help you stop this destructive behavior if you want to stop. Do not allow a grown boy or anything to keep you in this manner of destructive behavior, for it will only bring with it AIDS, low self-esteem, low self-worth, or maybe even death.

You are so valuable to Jesus, so start valuing yourself as He does. Jesus wants to help you with everything, and I mean everything you need. Your bill, rent, mortgage, groceries, car note, or whatever it is you need—seek Jesus, try Jesus, and give Him a chance to be the man who will show you the love you so desperately want, need, and desire. He is waiting on you to come to Him, and let me be the first to help you get to Him.

Repeat after me: Jesus, help me to leave my lifestyle of this destructive behavior that I am in. Help me to trust and depend on you. I may slip and fall again, but please forgive me and help me to get up and keep moving forward. I want to follow you and leave this part of my life in my past.

Show me your love and help me love myself the way you love me. Help me to value and see myself the way you value and see me. In Jesus's name I pray. Amen.

If you need to write this prayer down and read it every day until you see a change begin to take place in your life, do so. Read it daily or even throughout the day—whatever it takes to help you move forward.

Do not allow a grown boy to cheapen your worth after this chapter anymore. Remember, you are loved and your value is high, it reaches up to Heaven.

GIVE YOURSELF CREDIT

Women, we do not give ourselves credit. If we do give ourselves credit, I am sure it is not enough credit for the things we do, such as raising children, taking care of a family, and being a magician by stretching money far beyond its limits. We are the chauffeur, the referee, and the cook, just to mention a few things we do in a day's time.

Oh, I almost forgot how you also have to continue to look like a supermodel all day and be the love goddess in the bedroom. I want to take a few minutes and talk to you about your strengths. You are smart, intelligent, strong, loving, caring, and beautiful, and you have a lot to offer people. You may not think so, but you do.

I want you to name one thing that you are good at doing and think about how you could teach someone else to do it. You have something you are good at, even if you do not think so; I promise you that some woman would love you to teach her what you do well, and you may feel it is no big deal.

Women, we need to rally around each other, encourage one another, and show love toward each other more. You would be surprised to know how many women that I have hug said to me, "I have not had a hug in a long time."

One of the reasons why some women turn to these grown boys is for love or what they think is love. Women crave affection, passion, love, companionship, emotional support, and attention from a man. We have such big hearts, and we love hard when we do love. This is why it is so important for you to wait and allow God to lead the man to you.

We only get one life, and we want it filled with everything our heart desires along with the love from the man that God has chosen to love you and give you all those things in your life. You should have your little Heaven here on earth, and it can happen. You should not just settle for a grown boy.

Please, be patient enough to wait on God for what you deserve, want, and desire and for what you want God to give you. Go back, read the definition at the beginning of the book between a grown boy and a man, and see which one you want in your life. God never makes a mistake, and He longs to give you to a man who will love you the way

Jesus loves the church, and the last time I checked, Jesus really, really, really loves the church.

Start giving yourself more credit, and see yourself the way Jesus sees you—someone of value and of great worth. If this is hard for you to do, ask Jesus to show you how to love yourself the way He loves you. You were worth His sacrifice, so who are you to devalue yourself when He has placed such a high value on you that no one else can pay?

Honor what Jesus thinks of you and start thinking of yourself in that manner. Remember, what you think is very powerful, so think positive thoughts always. When you start to have negative thoughts about yourself, think of how Jesus sees you, and remember to give yourself credit because Jesus love you, so love yourself.

STOP DOING NOTHING

S top doing nothing sounds crazy, does it not? It will actually make sense when you finish reading this chapter. Many women are literally sitting around in their homes hoping, wishing, and praying for their life to change and for Prince Charming to just walk up and knock on their door or ring their doorbell. I will say this to you: good luck on that, and you need to stop doing nothing.

No one can see you through the walls of your house. In order for your Prince Charming or the man God wants to give you can find you, you must stop sitting around the house hoping, wishing, and praying he will knock on your door.

No, before you even ask, the deliveryman is not delivering himself to you, but it can happen that way. Now, women, do not start hitting on your deliveryman, okay? I did not say to do that.

Scripture does say that he who finds a wife finds a good thing and finds favor with God. See the word *find*? That means someone must be searching for something in order to find it. It did not say that he who goes knocking on women's doors will find her. If a man did that, he will be arrested for solicitation and being a stalker.

Now do you understand you must get up and get out the house so the man who is searching for you can find you? In the meanwhile, get yourself together. Whatever you need to do to prepare yourself for him—please start doing it now.

Put down the ice cream, start exercising, go to cooking classes, learn how to drive if you do not know how, and learn the art of communication if you need to.

Sometimes, women, you know you can throw the biggest pity parties, and you want everyone to feel sorry for you. Honey, please, the pity party club stops now. There will be no more excuses after reading this chapter, okay?

Start doing whatever it is you need to do to better your chances of getting a man's attention. Get off the couch, send up a smoke signal, and leave your house because no one can see you if you stay inside your house. Most importantly, stop doing nothing. Now does the title make sense to you? I thought it would.

CHILDREN COME FIRST

It is a shame that I have to write this chapter, but we must look out for and help the children. I know quite a few women who put a grown boy before their child or children, and this chapter is for you if you fall into this category.

To you I say, "Shame on you," and ask, "Are you crazy?" Grown boys come a dime a dozen, and your child or children are your responsibility to protect at all cost; they are to be first above all others. You have allowed this grown boy too much freedom in your home with your child or children.

Abuse, neglect, sexual assault, and even death have been the results of women putting these grown boys' needs ahead of their children's needs and safety. Children are innocent, and as their mother, you have an obligation and a responsibility to protect them at all cost.

Who is a grown boy that he should have the right to have his needs met before your child or children's needs? Some of you barely listen to your child or children, and they could be telling you something you need to know before it is too late.

Many of people have found themselves in so many of life situations such as alcoholism, drugs, and prostitution all because their mother placed a grown boy before them and never cared for them as a mother should.

If you know yourself to be a mother such as this, it is not too late to stop this life-changing and damaging behavior and turn things around with your child or children right now. If you are grown and this happened to you, please go out of your way to make sure this does not happen to your child or children.

If you have a child or children, please remember you must stop the old cycle and begin a new one, one of love and trust between you and your child or children where no grown boy comes before them.

If your child or children still live with you or are grown now, and your behavior placed them or has placed them in a situation to be hurt through abuse, neglect, or sexually assaulted—if it is not too late—please apologize to them for your either not listening or not believing them as a child. This caused their pain.

If you are grown and a product of a situation like this and have suffered because of it, it is now time to seek counseling and get the help you so desperately need to heal. Most importantly, you must first begin the healing process by forgiving the person or people who hurt you. Easier said than done, I am sure.

Nevertheless, you must forgive them so you can be free to start healing. Please, please, please I beg of you, put your child or children first in your life, and you will reap the most beautiful and wonderful harvest—a child's love for their mother.

JESUS IS YOUR MAN

I can stay on this chapter for days, but I will not. Jesus is the only man who shed His blood and died for you. Let me repeat that. Jesus is the only man who shed His blood and died for you. "Why did I repeat that?" some of you just asked. I will tell you why I repeated it.

Some of you women act, think, and expect a man to give you the sun, the moon, the stars, and his blood if need be to make you happy. You expect a man to go beyond his limits to prove himself to you, and this is why some of you are alone or about to be alone because you are pushing your man away.

Jesus is the only man who wanted to and did shed His blood to prove that He loves you with an everlasting love, so no matter what you do or have done, He will always love you. He gave you your worth and value when He died for you, so never think of yourself as worthless because you are so valuable that He gave His life for you. He has made you promises to take care of you and never leave you, and He keeps His promises; He will never break them.

Can you find a man who will make you promises and never break them? Some men out there can make you a promise and will not break it sometimes. Jesus will never break a promise to you. He is your provider no matter what you need.

He created a complete universe without your help, so your needs are not a problem for Him. You have only to ask and believe in faith that He will provide, and He will. You can talk to Him as long as you want and need to, and you will never talk too much for Him, for He is always ready to listen and has the best advice you can get.

He understands you, and you can be yourself (with or without make up, just a little humor). You do not have to worry about Him playing games with your feelings or your heart and mind, for He understands all your hurts and your fears. He sees all your tears and longs to comfort you.

Jesus is the man you are longing for. He is everything every woman needs, wants, and should desire. You must first love Him the way you desire to love a human man, and love Jesus more. You should long to be with and love Jesus the way you long to be with and love a human man.

Once you allow Jesus to be all you need, want, and desire, it is then that He will give you to the man that He created just for you. So wait on Jesus and love Him the way He loves you, and when He knows you are ready, He will then give you to the man of your dreams.

GIRL, WAKE UP

I wrote this book under the direction, guidance, and help of the Holy Spirit. This book is for God's daughters everywhere who need to wake up out of the slumber that we as women fall into sometimes, whether it is by our own doing or by some grown boy's doing.

I can only pray that you have read something in here that will at least get you thinking about changing your life for the better. You must first acknowledge the fact that you need to change some things in your life as we all do. It may or may not be easy to admit that you need help.

Nevertheless, help is something we all will need at some point in our lives. It takes a big person to admit they need help and to go about seeking to find help. Sometimes all we need is a push in the right direction to get started. I pray this book does this for you.

I want you to know that even though I may never meet all of you in person, I do want you to know that I will be praying for every woman who is reading this book. Please pass this book on to the next woman when you finish reading it, and if you think you need to hold on to it for future help, do so, but buy a second book and pass it on to a woman you know who needs it and will benefit from reading it.

Jesus is waiting to answer all your questions and be all you need Him to be for you. So pray, and get started on changing your life for the better for the rest of your life. I love you, and remember, you can do it. Jesus is waiting on you, so go get started and let today or tonight be the start of your new life.

ABOUT THE AUTHOR

Ms. Bernadette Bolden was born to Mr. Wheeler and Joyce Bolden on September 1, 1964. As one of eight children, she always possessed a nurturing spirit, which surpassed that of her siblings. As a young mother, she faced numerous daily struggles while raising her three children—Le'Shandra, Jh'Torre, and Ky'Vari Bolden.

Financial and emotional issues, a sense of abandonment by family members, and even the death of a brother were a few of the obstacles she had to face. However, Ms. Bernadette Bolden had one thing that would be the key to her forming a relationship with God. With God's help, conversations, and guidance of the Holy Spirit, Ms. Bernadette Bolden grew to become a strong African American woman with the wisdom of God deeply embedded inside her.

The journey you will embark upon as you read this book is one that will bring about a healing to you. Ms.

Bernadette Bolden wrote this book with the hope that it will uplift, strengthen, and encourage women everywhere to start right now and change their life for the better. No matter who you are or what path you are on in life, this book is for you the reader.

Please keep in mind that not every chapter in this book is for every woman reading it, but you will still learn something from every chapter as you read it with an open mind. Ms. Bernadette Bolden prays that you are empowered and inspired to move forward as the new woman you are to be in Jesus Christ.

CPSIA information can be obtained
at www.ICGtesting.com
Printed in the USA
BVHW031201080221
599623BV00008B/115